SAILING THE SEAWAYS

To Yvonne, Fionola and Peter

The Publication has received financial support from the Cultural Traditions Group of the Community Relations Council .

The Friar's Bush Press
24 College Park Avenue
BELFAST BT7 1LR

Published 1991
© Copyright reserved

ISBN 0 946872 45 7

Designed by Rodney Miller Associates, Belfast
Printed by W. & G. Baird, Antrim

·SAILING ·THE·SEAWAYS·

Historic maritime photographs from the
Ulster Folk and Transport Museum
1864-1939

Michael McCaughan

FRIAR'S BUSH PRESS

STRANGFORD, CO. DOWN, c.1865

This photograph is from one of the oldest glass plate negatives in the museum's collection. It was taken by the 24th Baron de Ros of Old Court, Strangford, an accomplished amateur photographer. As a royal equerry his photographic subjects included Queen Victoria and Prince Albert. Here he has framed three generations of seafarers in the doorway of his boathouse at Strangford. There is much of interest in the boatmen's clothes and their task of sewing a canvas sheath on a loop of rope to prevent chafing.

INTRODUCTION

Photography is an equation of light, space & time .... At its strongest, photography is the art of the real. Since its beginning the sheer fascination of the photograph has been with its nearness to reality, its perfection in delineation, its suggestion of absolute truthfulness ...
Peter Turner, The Meaning of Photography

Since the invention of photography over 150 years ago, photographs have become a most important source of visual information about the past. However, as with all types of evidence, historic photographs must not be accepted uncritically and should be interpreted in the light of other knowledge. Although they cannot explain the factors which shape the events of their day, photographs have the unique capacity to show us the appearance of things at a particular point in time. A fading snapshot or a modern print from an old negative can help us understand better the times to which they belonged. Photographs are unique and often evocative documents concerning events, people, places and things that can never be brought together in the same way again. They touch our sense of mortality by becoming markers of time's passage. It is this dimension of photography which partly explains the enduring popular appeal of historic photographs.

Views of maritime activity in Belfast were amongst the first outdoor photographs taken in Britain or Ireland. Using the daguerreotype process, Francis S. Beatty, a well known local engraver and photographic pioneer, recorded quayside shipping near the Old Long Bridge in August 1840. Alas these photographs (daguerreotypes) have not survived and indeed relatively few maritime photographs predate the 1880s. From this date onwards photography became cheaper, simpler and hence more popular. New processes, materials and equipment permitted greater mobility and allowed shorter exposure times, so not only did the number of photographers and photographs increase, but the range of pictures taken also became more varied. Henceforward it was possible for photographers to record virtually every aspect of the world in which they lived. Thousands of photographs were taken at home, in the country and in the streets; people were photographed in studios, on holiday, at leisure and at work. Reflecting contemporary pride in economic and technological progress, photographers were employed to record the latest engineering achievements, from railway locomotives to ocean liners. In Ulster, the major industries were documented in detail, notably by R.J. Welch and W.A. Green. In particular, Harland and Wolff commissioned Welch to photograph the building of ships at Queen's Island, their works having become one of the world's leading shipyards. Many other aspects of maritime activity were photographed by professionals and amateurs alike. Their surviving prints and negatives, taken around the Ulster coast and at sea, now form a vivid visual record of the major changes that occurred in the technology and organisation of water transport in the late nineteenth and early twentieth centuries.

This book is not a history of seafaring under sail in Ulster using old photographs. It is simply a chronological presentation of historic maritime photographs with explanatory captions. The linking theme is man's encounter with the sea, and his harnessing of the wind's power to propel ships and boats for fishing and trade. Yachting photographs are not included. The geographical emphasis is on the northern coasts of Ireland and the sea-ways connecting our shores to the wider world.

The photographs have been selected from the museum's extensive photographic archive. Some are from major collections of glass plate negatives, while others, no less important, have been taken from old prints loaned or donated to the museum. Maritime photographs have been collected over a long period of time. The earliest acquisitions date from the founding years of the museum more than a quarter of a century ago. Other photographs in the book have been lodged in the archive within the past few months. The task of expanding the collection and increasing its comprehensiveness, is a continuing responsibility. It is hoped that this publication will bring the maritime aspect of the photographic archive to a wider public. Perhaps it will also encourage readers to make their historic photographs available to the museum for preservation, study, and enjoyment.

Michael McCaughan
Ulster Folk & Transport Museum, 1991

GLENARM, CO. ANTRIM, c.1870

Dr John Sinclair Holden was a general practitioner who lived in Glenarm 1867-72. As an amateur photographer he made an early and valuable photographic record of shipping in the local harbours. Here he stands in his sailing boat, humorously called THE EMETIC.

GLENARM, CO. ANTRIM, c.1870

Limestone was the staple export from the harbour, which was in course of improvement when Dr Holden took this photograph. Small trading vessels lie alongside the quays at low water. On the left, one of them is drying its mainsail, and to prevent an accidental capsize, a securing line has been run from the mast to the quayside. In the foreground the distinctive full-bodied hulls of Scottish gabbarts reflect long-standing sea-borne links between the Glens of Antrim and the west of Scotland.

CARNLOUGH, CO. ANTRIM, c.1870

The harbour was built in 1854 by the Marchioness of Londonderry to facilitate the shipping of limestone from estate quarries. A tramway system enabled stone to be loaded directly into the holds of ships by means of overhead chutes. Here two bluff-bowed vessels - a smack and a 2-masted schooner - are waiting to take their place at the loading berth adjacent to the smack drying its topsail.

RED BAY, CO. ANTRIM, c.1870
Cushendall and Waterfoot were served by the pier at Red Bay. At this date its principal trade was the export of iron ore from newly established mines in the local hinterland. With about 17 feet of water at spring tides, relatively large vessels could be berthed at the pier. Here a schooner, a brigantine and a recently built 3-masted schooner contrast with the smack in the foreground, with its single mast and old-fashioned hull.

CARRICKFERGUS, CO. ANTRIM, 1864

This is the work of a professional photographer recording the latest wooden sailing ship turned out by Carrickfergus Shipyard. She is the 350 ton clipper brig CATHERINE FULLERTON, designed and built in 1864 by the talented shipyard manager, Paul Rodgers. Her lofty masts appear to tower over the twelfth century Norman castle, while her yacht-like hull contrasts with surrounding vessels.

CARRICKFERGUS SHIPYARD, CO. ANTRIM, 1870

Paul Rodgers become proprietor of Carrickfergus Shipyard in 1870 when this photograph was taken. A wooden barque, employed in the foreign trade, has been hauled out for repair and refitting on the slipway. The full-bodied, deep, narrow hull is characteristic of wooden sailing ships built in the first half of the nineteenth century. In the background a small vessel, the cutter yacht VENTURE, is under construction.

KILKEEL, CO. DOWN, 1876

The first pier was completed in 1868, and subsequently improved, in order to help establish Kilkeel as an important herring fishery station. Between 1870 and 1880 the local fleet increased by 100 per cent, with a peak of 24 first class boats in 1877. The harbour was also used by trading vessels, notably for the export of granite.

KILKEEL BOATYARD, CO. DOWN, 1876
This is an enlarged detail of the previous photograph, showing a new boatyard being laid out by
the Cornishman, William Paynter. He had come from St Ives in 1875 to build West Cornish
luggers, which were in great demand by Irish Sea fishermen for the off-shore herring and mackerel
fisheries. The fine-lined hull of a Cornish lugger can be seen on the left. The boilerhouse in
course of construction here was destroyed by fire in November 1876.

CELTIC AT QUEEN'S ISLAND, BELFAST, 1872

From the early 1870s Harland & Wolff commissioned professional photographs of many of the iron ships built at Queen's Island. Here the trans-Atlantic steamship CELTIC is almost ready for delivery in October 1872. At this time the shipyard was establishing its reputation for constructing high quality ships of advanced design. Nevertheless, sails were still required to augment steam propulsion, especially on long ocean voyages, or to replace the engine entirely in the event of mechanical failure.

MAJESTIC, BELFAST, 1875

For many years Harland & Wolff built both steamships and deep water sailing ships. The latter could offer competitive freight rates and be operated profitably in specialist long distance trades. The iron full-rigged ship MAJESTIC was completed in June 1875 for the Liverpool firm T. & J. Brocklebank. She represents the highest development of the square-rigged merchant sailing ship at this period.

CELTIC, BELFAST, 1872
View forward from the ship's navigating bridge. Note the standard compass and the foremast with
its combination of furled square sails and fore-and-aft sails.

MAJESTIC, BELFAST, 1875
The elegant clipper bow and handsome figure-head of MAJESTIC contrast with the functional straight stem of the steamship CELTIC. The spars projecting forward from the stem are the bowsprit and jib-boom. They are important in the masting and rigging arrangements of a sailing ship. The overlapping lines of riveted iron hull plates, or strakes, can be clearly seen.

CELTIC, BELFAST, 1872
View aft towards the ship's navigating bridge, wheelhouse, mainmast and funnel. Particularly
striking is the complex system of standing rigging which supports the masts and spars, and the
running rigging by which the sails, bent to the spars, are controlled.

CELTIC, BELFAST, 1872
View of the steamship's port bow. The two seamen standing beside the furled headsails contrast
with the massive iron anchor secured to the deck.

GERMANIC, BELFAST, 1875

This ship was completed by Harland & Wolff in April 1875 for the White Star Line's Liverpool/New York service. With a long narrow hull characteristic of H &W-built steamships, she represents the leading edge of shipbuilding technology of her day. In February 1876 GERMANIC won the eastbound Atlantic speed crossing with a passage of 7 days 15 hours and 17 minutes at an average speed of 15.79 knots. She could carry 220 passengers in first class and 1500 in third class.

MAJESTIC, BELFAST, 1875

A stern view of the ship whose stately appearance aptly reflects her name. The bold sheerline of the hull and the tall raking masts are characteristic of the sailing ships which were built by Harland & Wolff until 1890. Note the position of the ship's wheel on the poop deck above the rudder. In contrast to the steamship CELTIC's weather-protected wheelhouse amidships, the helmsman of MAJESTIC was entirely exposed to the wind and the sea.

STRANGFORD, CO DOWN, c.1885
The work of loading a small sail trader with a cargo of potatoes, using wheelbarrows and chutes, has stopped for the photographer. The blurred figures are those who moved during the long exposure time. The wooden schooner VISION was built in 1867 at Garmouth in Scotland. In the mid 1880s she was owned by John Ternan of Skerries, Co. Dublin.

STRANGFORD, CO DOWN, c.1885

This is an ancient port whose former economic and military significance was considerable. In the 1880s coal was the chief import and potatoes the main export. A charge of 2d per ton register was made on vessels discharging. This favoured ships of small tonnage. The wooden schooner on the right, WILD WAVE was 69 registered tons, so her dues amounted to 11/6d (57½p).

STRANGFORD, CO DOWN, c.1885

A schooner has sunk close to the quay, to which it is secured by lines. Another schooner lies off, with her gaffs lowered and the fore and main sails gathered in, to prevent a breeze from filling them. However the water appears calm and a diver is working on the sunken vessel from a small boat.

BELFAST, c.1881

By the 1880s Belfast had developed as a major port, with an annual trade figure of about 2 million tons. Vessels entering the port were engaged in both the foreign and home trades. Here a handsome coastal schooner is drying her sails, while in the background a steam paddle tug lies alongside an ocean-going wooden barque. The foreground is dominated by the counter stern of a yawl-rigged yacht. This photograph, and others of Belfast shipping in the 1880s, was taken by William Swanston, a gifted amateur photographer and a leading member of the Belfast Natural History and Philosophical Society.

BELFAST, c.1881
The importation of coal was essential for an industrial city without a native supply of fuel.
Hundreds of small sailing vessels were engaged in the cross-channel coal trade. The majority were
brigantines, like these vessels moored in Victoria Channel convenient to the coal quays on the Co.
Down side of the River Lagan. The MARY ELLEN, with her sails partly furled, was built in 1857
and owned by the coal merchant Alexander King.

BELFAST, c.1881

Three wooden sailing colliers moored in Victoria Channel contrast with cross-channel iron-built steamships alongside Donegall Quay. Coal is being discharged into a lighter from the brigantine in the foreground. The brigantine on the left, the CAPRIOLE, was built in Prince Edward Island in 1858 and owned by J. S. Bell of Islandmagee until 1882.

BELFAST, c.1881
The importation of timber, particularly from Canada, was an important part of the foreign trade of
the port. Many Belfast timber merchants were also shipowners and their large ocean-going sailing
ships regularly crossed the Atlantic. The wooden barque OCEAN was typical of these vessels,
many of which were built in Canada. She was built in Nova Scotia in 1863 and owned by T.
Dixon & Sons until 1881. The wooden paddle tug VICTOR was owned by H. Quinn and built in
Middlesborough, also in 1863.

BELFAST, c.1881
Two wooden paddle tugs, VICTOR and RANGER, lie alongside a wooden barque which has discharged its cargo of Canadian timber. Like the majority of vessels in this trade, she is North American-built.

WORKMAN CLARK & COMPANY, BELFAST, 1887

The shipbuilding firm of Workman Clark & Company was established in 1880 on the Co. Antrim side of the River Lagan. The sailing ship DERBY PARK is being fitted out after her launch, while the two Londonderry-registered steamers, MOUNTJOY and FAUGH-A-BALLAGH, have probably come to the yard for repair.

DERBY PARK, BELFAST, 1887
For the final stage of fitting out the steel barque DERBY PARK has been dry docked in the
Hamilton Graving Dock. Men can be seen on a yard bending a sail. She was completed in 1887
for Peter Iredale and Son, Liverpool.

BRITISH MERCHANT, 1880

The iron full-rigger BRITISH MERCHANT was completed in October 1880 by Harland & Wolff for British Shipowners Limited, Liverpool. On her maiden voyage she sailed from Liverpool to Melbourne in 77 days, crossed the Pacific from Newcastle, New South Wales to San Francisco in 55 days, and came home round the Horn to Queenstown in 101 days. She arrived on 19 September 1881, after 10 months and 16 days.

LORD TEMPLETOWN AT SAN FRANCISCO, c.1888

Built in 1886 by Harland & Wolff for the Irish Shipowners' Company Limited, Belfast (T. Dixon & Sons, managers), LORD TEMPLETOWN had the distinction of being the largest barque-rigged vessel in the world. She was employed in the North American bulk cargo trade, and particularly in the Californian grade trade. Here she is at anchor in San Francisco Bay, photographed by the marine photographer Thomas H. Wilton.

STAR OF RUSSIA VOYAGE, 1882

The Star Line of iron clipper ships owned by James P. Corry & Company of Belfast was one of the most famous fleets of the nineteenth century. All were built in Belfast and were engaged in the Calcutta and Australian trades. The STAR OF RUSSIA was delivered by Harland & Wolff in February 1875 and was one of the finest full-rigged sailing ships of her day. In 1882 William Corry, a keen amateur photographer, made a convalescent voyage in STAR OF RUSSIA to Calcutta, and a number of his photographs have survived. This splendid view of STAR OF RUSSIA was taken from the ship's boat during a period of calm weather.

STAR OF RUSSIA VOYAGE, 1882
View aft from the forecastle deck. One of the innovative features of the ship was the combining of
the iron lower masts and top masts. Men on the yards have gathered in the foresail and mainsail to
provide an unimpeded view for the photographer.

STAR OF RUSSIA VOYAGE, 1882

This is Captain John Simpson reading in his book-lined panelled cabin in the after part of the ship under the poop deck. He can communicate with the officer of the watch through a speaking tube. A cat is asleep in his berth. Photographs were rarely taken below decks on sailing ships.

STAR OF RUSSIA VOYAGE, 1882
Other passengers bound for Calcutta pose for the photographer. It is possible that the man in the white hat facing away from the camera is William Corry. The young boy is sitting astride a signal cannon.

STAR OF RUSSIA VOYAGE, 1882
An informal portrait of Captain Simpson sitting on the poop deck with his pet dog. It was not unusual for a shipmaster to wear a civilian suit and a bowler hat. The photograph shows interesting details of the standing and running rigging.

STAR OF RUSSIA VOYAGE, 1882

On a sailing ship the crew was divided into two groups, the port watch and the starboard watch. This is a posed photograph, taken in fair weather, with both watches furling the mainsail. Nevertheless it dramatically illustrates how seamen worked aloft handling heavy canvas sails. In foul weather the ship would be pitching and rolling. Each man would have one arm for the ship and one arm for himself.

CREW OF FINGAL, c.1888
This formal portrait of the master, officers and crew of the 4-masted barque FINGAL was taken in San Francisco by the professional marine photographer Thomas H. Wilton. The arrangement and dress of the men suggests the authority and social structure on board the ship. FINGAL was built by Harland & Wolff in 1883 for Richard Martin & Company, Dublin.

COPTIC, 1881

In contrast to the casually dressed seamen of the sailing ship FINGAL, the crew of the White Star steamship COPTIC are formally dressed in a uniform supplied by the company. The photograph was taken when the ship was nearing completion in Belfast. The man in the bowler hat is probably a Harland & Wolff employee.

DORIC, BELFAST, 1883
When this passenger/cargo steamship was built by Harland & Wolff in 1883, the transition from auxiliary sail to wholly steam propulsion was still not complete. In 1891 Rudyard Kipling took passage in DORIC to New Zealand. Her dour chief engineer, Mr R. Reid, is thought to have been Kipling's inspiration for 'McAndrew's Hymn'.

BELFAST, 1887

This photograph has a symbolic quality. It was taken on 17 September 1887, following the launch of the Harland & Wolff-built steamship OCEANA. She is being towed up Victoria Channel to be completed at a fitting out berth. In the background a forest of sailing ship masts stand out against the Belfast Mountains. As the steel hull of OCEANA moves into view there is a wonderful juxtaposition of new and old, metal and wood, steam and sail. The photograph is a powerful expression of technological change and the advent of a new order.

DUNDRUM, CO. DOWN, c.1885

By the 1880s innovations in industrial technology were not confined to large ports. In Dundrum the cross-channel services of the East Downshire Steamship Company were connected to wider markets by railway tracks running directly to the quayside. Here these improvements in transportation are thrown into relief by the abandoned sailing ship GRACE. Built in 1818 at Lytham in Lancashire, she has a deep, full-bodied hull typical of the period. Rigged as a brigantine, GRACE worked in the Irish Sea trades until c.1882.

CARRICKFERGUS SHIPYARD, CO. ANTRIM, 1887

Paul Rodgers, proprietor of the shipyard, was a famous designer and builder of small merchant sailing ships. He specialised in schooner construction and was one of the few small-scale shipbuilders who made the technological change from wood to metal shipbuilding. This photograph was taken on 24 September 1887. On the left, wooden schooners are being repaired on the patent ship and in the dry dock. To the right, the steel 3-masted schooner PATRICIAN is nearing completion on the stocks. Her masts have been fitted before launching. With her fine lines and sweeping sheer, PATRICIAN is a typical Paul Rodgers' metal schooner.

CARRICKFERGUS SHIPYARD, CO. ANTRIM, 1887

Various individuals pose for the photographer on 24 September 1887. The wooden schooner ELIZABETH ELLEN FISHER is on the patent slip being recaulked. This was a regular requirement for wooden vessels in order to minimise hull leakage. Caulking consists of stuffing the seams (spaces between the planking) with oakum and then 'paying' or coating them with hot pitch. In the background the steel 3-masted schooner PATRICIAN is almost ready for launching.

CARRICKFERGUS SHIPYARD, CO. ANTRIM, 1885
This photograph was commissioned to mark the building of one of Paul Rodgers' first metal-hulled ships. The change from wood, to iron and steel shipbuilding at Carrickfergus took place in 1885. Besides investment in new equipment, new skills had to be learnt. Here the entire workforce of about 100 hands display pride and achievement. Paul Rodgers is standing in the back row, third from the left, wearing a bowler hat.

RESULT, CARRICKFERGUS, CO. ANTRIM, 1893

The steel 3-masted topsail schooner RESULT was the last merchant sailing ship to be built at Carrickfergus Shipyard. When completed in 1893 for owners in north west England, she represented the highest technical development of the coastal schooner. Designed by Paul Rodgers to be a functional yet graceful vessel, RESULT became one of the best known and most successful schooners in the coastal and home trades. In modified form she continued to carry cargoes until 1967, by which time she was the last vessel of her type still working in British and Irish waters. RESULT was acquired for preservation by the Ulster Folk and Transport Museum in 1970.

WORKFORCE OF CARRICKFERGUS SHIPYARD, CO. ANTRIM, c.1896

Due to financial difficulties, Paul Rodgers was forced to sell the shipyard in 1892, but managed to repurchase it in 1895. However there was no demand for new schooners and the yard concentrated on ship repair. The much reduced workforce, mainly shipwrights, was photographed c.1896. Paul Rodgers, standing on the left, remained in active business until his death in 1901.

CALIFORNIA, 4-MASTED BARQUE, 1890

In the 1880s and 90s, as world trade expanded and competition from steamships increased, ocean going sailing ships were designed to combine greater carrying capacity with economy of operation. Steel hulls became longer, and the 4-masted barque was developed as an efficient carrier of bulk cargoes in deep water trades. The 3099 ton CALIFORNIA, built by Harland & Wolff in 1890, was one of the finest vessels of her day, but sadly she was also the last sailing ship built at Queen's Island.

POLTALLOCH, BELFAST, c.1895

Built in 1893 by Workman & Company, the 4-masted barque POLTALLOCH towers above the dockside square-sets after a deepwater voyage. Her steel hull, masts and spars are products of industrial shipbuilding and contrast with the older timber-built barque in the background. With all new ship orders being for steamships, the building of sailing ships in Belfast ceased in 1896.

SAIL LOFT, HARLAND & WOLFF, 1899

Despite the end of sailing ship building in Belfast, sails were still required by some steamship owners or by vessels in for refitting. In the shipyard sail loft, canvas cloths were cut to pattern on the wooden floor, before being machine stitched together to form a completed sail.

RIGGING SHED, HARLAND & WOLFF, 1899
The rigging shed, like the sail loft, was a necessary and important part of the shipyard infrastructure. Here riggers prepared the standing and running rigging which supported ships' masts and controlled the spars. They were skilled in working both heavy wire and natural fibre rigging.

HAMILTON GRAVING DOCK, BELFAST, c.1899

In this contrast of technologies, the wooden barque BELFAST is undergoing repairs against the backdrop of steel shipbuilding at Queen's Island. Registered at Grimstad, Norway, she was built as the EDWARD D. JEWETT at Portland, New Brunswick in 1871. Interestingly a windmill has been fitted on the poop deck, for the operation of the ship's pumps.

WILLIAM MITCHELL, FULL-RIGGED SHIP, c.1892

In addition to a long tradition of shipowning, the port of Londonderry was a successful shipbuilding centre in the late nineteenth century. From 1882-92, W. F. Bigger's Foyle Shipyard specialised in the construction of big sailing ships. The 2035 ton full-rigger WILLIAM MITCHELL, was the largest and also the last vessel to come from the yard. Built for the Derry ship-owner, William Mitchell, in 1892, she traded under different owners until 1927. By this date WILLIAM MITCHELL had become the last working full-rigged ship to fly the red ensign.

WRECK OF THE ULRICA, COPELAND ISLANDS, 1897

In a January gale in 1897, the iron 4-masted ship ULRICA ran aground on the Old Lighthouse Island at the entrance to Belfast Lough. Bound from San Francisco to Dublin with a cargo of grain, she became a total loss, although her crew of 28 all landed safely. ULRICA was built on the Clyde in 1884 and made her best run the following year when she sailed 370 miles in 24 hours while on passage from London to Sydney.

WRECK OF THE ULRICA, 1897
There is a poignancy about this view aft towards the submerged stern of the stricken ship. The
lifeboats have gone from their skids and ULRICA has been abandoned to the wind and the sea.

BRIGANTINE OFF BELFAST LOUGH c.1898

Square-rigged on the foremast, and fore and aft rigged on the main, brigantines were employed in both the foreign and home trades. This unidentified brigantine is built of wood and her masts and sails are well proportioned. Many were built in Canada and vessels of this rig were favoured by shipowners engaged in the Belfast coal trade.

SCHOONER OFF BELFAST LOUGH c.1898

With relatively low capital and operating costs, schooners became increasingly common in the second half of the nineteenth century. They were fore and aft rigged, with square topsails on the foremast. Hundreds of 2 and 3-masted schooners were profitably employed in the coastal and home trades until well into the present century. This small wooden schooner contrasts with the larger iron and steel schooners turned out by Carrickfergus Shipyard. Its distinctive stern and rudder are characteristic of Irish Sea schooners built in north west England.

MAGHERAMORNE, CO. ANTRIM, c.1898
The pier at Magheramorne in Larne Lough was used for the loading of lime and limestone from
the nearby quarry. Here a schooner lies alongside the pier where there was 12 feet of water at
spring tides. Another schooner is anchored offshore waiting its turn to load.

ROSTREVOR, CO. DOWN, c.1898

Three schooners at Rostrevor in Carlingford Lough reflect the importance of small sailing vessels in the economy and trade of coastal communities. A cargo of potatoes is being loaded from horse-drawn carts into the schooner at the head of the pier. She is the VILLAGE BELLE, 95 tons, built in Barnstaple, Devon in 1878 and owned in Skerries, Co. Dublin.

QUOILE RIVER, CO. DOWN, c.1897

From early times the picturesque River Quoile was used by shipping serving the historic town of Downpatrick. In the late nineteenth century, imports were coal, timber and salt and the exports mainly potatoes and grain. Here a ketch lies alongside Steamboat Quay, built in the late 1830s, a mile downstream from the main Quoile Quay. Just as schooners were more economical to build and operate than brigs and brigantines, so ketch-rigged vessels were cheaper than schooners.

QUEEN'S QUAY, BELFAST, c.1895
In the mid 1890s, sailing colliers, mainly brigantines, still outnumbered steamboats in the Belfast coal trade. In this unusual photograph, coal is being bagged on board colliers at the quayside and loaded directly on to horse-drawn wagons for city distribution.

BARQUENTINES, BELFAST LOUGH, c.1898

(Above)

Barquentines were distinctively square-rigged on the foremast and fore and aft rigged on the main and mizzen masts. The rig was developed on the west coast of North America in the mid-nineteenth century for the economical operation of ocean-going sailing ships. Several barquentines, very similar to this unidentified vessel, were built at Carrickfergus Shipyard between 1882 and 1891.

(Opposite)

A wooden barquentine, probably North American-built, heels to starboard as she is towed towards Belfast by a steam paddle tug. Tugs were required to bring large sailing vessels into the port.

VICTORIA CHANNEL AND QUEEN'S ISLAND, BELFAST, 1895
The vessels in this photograph reflect the nineteenth century changes in shipbuilding technology, from wood to metal and from sail to steam. Symbolically the wooden schooner and the steel 4-masted barque are dominated by steamships, especially the huge steel hull of the GEORGIC under construction by Harland and Wolff.

STEAM AND SAIL, BELFAST LOUGH, 1900

By 1900 the now mechanically efficient steamship had superseded the wind-driven ship as the main form of ocean transport. In the United Kingdom almost all new shipbuilding orders were for steam tonnage. The supremacy of the steamship is suggested in this photograph of the MINNEWASKA, after completion by Harland and Wolff in March 1900. However many sailing ships, especially those in the coastal trade, continued to earn profits for their owners until well into the twentieth century.

GREENCASTLE YAWLS, BURTONPORT, CO. DONEGAL, c.1905
In the latter part of the nineteenth century, fishermen in west Donegal began to replace their old heavy boat types with new sailing and pulling boats, known as Greencastle yawls. Double-ended and clinker-built, they were a regional variation of a type of open fishing boat characteristic of the north and east coasts of Ireland. Yawls were not built at Burtonport, but were sailed or rowed from boatbuilding yards in Portrush, Co. Antrim and Moville, near Greencastle in east Donegal.

NEAR BURTONPORT, CO. DONEGAL, c.1905
Here some of the crew of a Greencastle yawl are rowing their boat through Duck Sound between Rutland and Duck Islands. To help the oarsmen, a simple working rig of spritsail and foresail has been set to catch the light airs. Yawls were about 22-24 feet in length and were light enough to be hauled ashore on exposed coasts where harbour accommodation was limited.

NEAR BURTONPORT, CO. DONEGAL, c.1905

This is an interesting photograph of a Greencastle yawl, in a good sailing breeze, with its distinctive rig of two spritsails and a jib. In 1890 a fishery inspector reported that '... *along the Donegal coast, Greencastle yawls, clinker-built, sharp at both ends, light fast and weatherly, usually painted white or red lead and costing about £11 fully found, are rapidly taking the place of the old boats ... when loaded with nets or fish they float lighter than the wall sided boat; and from their sharp pointed ends will make better weather when running or when head to sea ...*'

SAILING A GREENCASTLE YAWL, NEAR BURTONPORT, CO. DONEGAL, c.1905
Like the other Burtonport photographs, this remarkable view on board a yawl under sail, is from
the collection of Everina Maxwell, who lived on Inniscoo Island. In addition to her photographic
skills she was an able boatwoman and for many years was the Honorary Secretary of Aranmore
lifeboat station. Everina Maxwell is at the helm of the boat, seated directly behind the bearded
Captain John O'Donnell, also of Inniscoo Island.

YAWL LISSEY, GROOMSPORT, CO. DOWN, c.1901

Unlike west Donegal, the double-ended, clinker-built open boat was a long established type on the coast of Co. Down. At Groomsport, at the mouth of Belfast Lough, yawls were used for longline fishing and also for pilot work. Measuring up to 32 feet in length, the larger yawls were rigged with two dipping lugsails, and oars were used as necessary. LISSEY was photographed c.1901 prior to making a passage to Port Patrick in Scotland in the record time of 2 hours 40 minutes.

FISHERMEN, GROOMSPORT, CO. DOWN, c.1906
Longline fishing for cod was a winter occupation, with men sailing and rowing their yawls up to 10 miles to the fishing grounds. The photograph does not reveal the cold and arduous nature of the work, although it does suggest the importance of family and kinship in close-knit coastal communities. In the summer months it was common for some fishermen to work as paid hands in local yachts.

YAWL, COPELAND ISLAND, CO. DOWN, c.1910

Prior to 1912, many of the yawls at Groomsport and Donaghadee were built by James Emerson, whose family lived on the Big Isle of the Copeland Islands. This is probably a newly-built yawl, as everything has been neatly arranged for the photograph, from the sails and rigging, to James Emerson at the tiller of the boat. With its double-ended shape and clinker hull construction of overlapping planks, this yawl is in the same ancient European boatbuilding tradition as the Viking longships of 1000 years ago.

YAWL LUCY, DONAGHADEE, CO. DOWN, 1901
During a severe storm on 7 November 1901, the German barque MERIDIAN got into difficulties off Donaghadee. In terrible conditions local fishermen rendered assistance in the 21 ft yawl LUCY. Afterwards the launch was re-enacted specially for the photographer. The masts and spars of the MERIDIAN have been pencilled-in in the background.

PORTAVOGIE NOBBYS OFF BANGOR, CO. DOWN, c.1905

This early photograph of Portavogie 'nobbys' under sail nicely illustrates the particular type of lug-rigged herring drifter characteristic of this Co. Down fleet. Setting a jib sail and standing lugsails on both fore and mizzen masts, the nobby evolved in the Isle of Man in the early 1880s and was soon adopted by Portavogie fishermen. Many Portavogie nobbys were built in Manx yards, but in the mid 1880s William Mahood established a local boatyard and continued to build nobbys until the first world war.

PORTAVOGIE NOBBYS, ARDGLASS, CO. DOWN, c.1901

Portavogie fishing boats, like those from other localities, worked out of Ardglass during the summer herring season. This view of nobbys at the quayside provides a great deal of evidence about their design, construction and rigging arrangements. Most of them are second-class boats under 15 tons, with crew accommodation forward beneath the half deck.

HERRING FLEET, ARDGLASS, CO. DOWN, c.1901

Due to its proximity to the fishing grounds and because it could be entered at all states of the tide, Ardglass was the major Ulster port for the Irish Sea herring fishery. In peak years hundreds of fishing boats from the east coast of Ireland, from Scotland, the Isle of Man and Cornwall landed their catches here. The fleet in this photograph mainly comprises Portavogie nobbys, but also includes fast sailing Cornish-style luggers or 'nickeys'. All these boats were characterised by the 2-masted lug rig and they contrast with the old fashioned smack whose single mast has been lowered by its crew.

TRAWLERS OFF BELFAST LOUGH, CO. DOWN, c.1901

In the early nineteenth century, single-masted gaff-rigged smacks were common, not only as fishing craft, but also as small merchant ships. By 1900, on the north and east coasts of Ireland, the rig was confined largely to sailing trawlers, such as these boats working out of Groomsport. It was a very handy rig, yet powerful enough to pull heavy trawl nets through the water. The smack in the foreground does not have her trawl down, and her gaff mainsail has been triced or drawn up to lose the wind.

TRAWLERS, PORTSTEWART, CO. LONDONDERRY, c.1905

Onlookers watch with interest as the decked trawler CE187 is manoeuvred out of the confined space of the small harbour. Her gaff mainsail has been set ready for sea and the jib has been partly hoisted. At her stern the skipper is pushing off the bowsprit of another trawler. These boats are clinker-built and many are distinguished by a handsome clipper bow.

TRAWLER, PORTRUSH, CO. ANTRIM, c.1909
This scene, close to the shore, has probably been arranged by the photographer, W. A. Green, to demonstrate a local gaff-rigged trawler working under sail. Despite its large sail area, the yacht-like trawler is making very little headway. This has been achieved by the set of the sails in relation to the wind.

SCHOONER CHARLES, VICTORIA CHANNEL, BELFAST, c.1910
These two views of the wooden topsail schooner CHARLES are from 'real photograph' postcards privately published by J. J., 24 William Street South, Belfast. Postmarked in the summer of 1910, they depict a smart and well maintained vessel earning a living for her owners and crew in the coastal trade.

SCHOONER CHARLES, VICTORIA CHANNEL, BELFAST, c.1910
The CHARLES was built in 1871 by W. C. Paynter & Company in the port of Amlwch, in
Anglesey, North Wales. She was lost during the first world war.

SCHOONER BUSY BEE, ANNALONG, CO. DOWN, c.1910

Annalong, well known for its narrow harbour entrance, was a small but significant port for sailing vessels engaged in the export of potatoes and Mourne granite. Local investment in shipping increased markedly after 1880. By 1900, 14 sailing vessels, mainly schooners, totalling 762 tons were owned in Annalong. The BUSY BEE, like all the others, was bought second hand, and when a local man, Alex Gordon, took this photograph, she was 46 years old.

ANNALONG, CO DOWN, c.1904
The scale of Annalong's trade at the beginning of the century is suggested in this photograph. The basin is choked full of schooners and ketches, their full-bodied hulls built to take the ground in tidal harbours. Slabs of granite are stacked on the quayside and on board the NYMPH, the crew's washing has been hung out to dry.

ANNALONG, CO. DOWN, c.1915

The maritime economy of Annalong related to fishing as well as to trade. Here locally-owned fishing boats, mainly nobbys, contrast with the Scottish-registered ketch CHRISTINE SHEARER loading a cargo of granite and potatoes. The deck of the nickey HONEY BEE is in the foreground. Built at Peel in the Isle of Man in 1889, she was bought from Portavogie owners in 1910 by John Heaney and her skipper George Nugent. On 30 May 1918, HONEY BEE was sunk by a German submarine, together with ten other Co. Down fishing boats.

KILKEEL, CO. DOWN, c.1917

From the completion of the first pier in 1868, Kilkeel harbour was continuously expanded and improved, to accommodate large numbers of boats attending the Irish Sea herring fishery. With considerable local investment, the Kilkeel fishing fleet became the largest in Ulster. Trading vessels were also owned in Kilkeel, although the schooners and ketches in this photograph belonged to other ports. Their regular outward cargoes were granite and potatoes, together with barrels of cured herring.

CREW OF PHILLIS, ANNALONG, c.1914
Unusually the photographer has included himself in this picture of the skipper and crew of the Annalong schooner PHILLIS. All are local men, but Alex 'Manchie' Gordon (left), the photographer, is wearing a suit and can be distinguished easily from the group of seamen. From the left they are, Willie Hill, Captain Charlie Gordon, Joe Trimble and Topsy Gordon. PHILLIS was built in Preston in 1860.

CREW OF WILLIAM AND MARGARET, ANNALONG, c.1918

The majority of schooners owned in Annalong and Kilkeel retained the port of registry of their previous owners. WILLIAM AND MARGARET's lifebuoy shows that she was registered in Dublin and the flags indicate the allegiance of her crew. From the left they are, Sammy Agnew, Charlie McBurney (mate), Captain Tommy McBurney, and West Lyttle. The WILLIAM AND MARGARET was broken-up at Annalong c.1922.

KETCH, ANNALONG, CO. DOWN, c.1915

This wooden ketch, possibly the ST AUDELL, is on the port tack, as the wind is filling her heavily patched sails on the port or left side. Probably she has just cleared the harbour as her fenders are still out. However she is sailing without a cargo and much of her unladen hull is exposed as she heels to starboard.

LOADING A SCHOONER, PORTAVOGIE, CO. DOWN, c.1912

This remarkable photograph incorporates a great deal of social and technical information, ranging from the women helping to load sacks of potatoes, to the fittings and rigging of the wooden schooner. She is the GEORGE AND MARY, bought from Jersey owners in 1908 by Captain William Hughes of Portavogie. On 4 June 1915, GEORGE AND MARY was sunk by a German submarine off the coast of Co. Mayo, while carrying a cargo of scrap iron. Captain Hughes, his son Johnny and the other two crew members were saved.

KETCHES, PORTAFERRY, CO. DOWN, c.1912

The professional photographer, W. A. Green, made a remarkable visual record of everyday life in Ulster between c.1910 and 1940. Here he has photographed coastal trading vessels at Portaferry before new methods of transport and distribution brought about their eventual extinction. The ketch in the foreground, the AZUR, was built in Jersey in 1871, and was worked by local Co. Down owners from 1903 to 1928.

SCHOONER MAYFLOWER, PORTAFERRY, CO. DOWN, c.1912

Until the advent of motor lorries, relatively isolated coastal communities, like Portaferry and the Upper Ards, depended largely on small sailing vessels for the transportation of goods. Schooners and ketches supplied Portaferry and district with such diverse cargoes as coal, timber, bricks and slates, together with flour, groceries, farm implements and seeds. Outward cargoes were mainly grain and potatoes. The 60 ton schooner MAYFLOWER, built in 1874, was owned by James Ross of Islandmagee, though registered at Stranraer.

CARNLOUGH, CO. ANTRIM, c.1912

When this photograph was taken by W. A. Green, wooden sailing vessels were no longer being built in Britain or Ireland. However many older schooners and ketches continued to work profitably in the coastal and home trades, despite competition from steam coasters. Here the Carnlough Lime Company's S.S. OLDERFLEET contrasts with the 55 ton wooden ketch MILL BAY, owned in the Ards, Co. Down. Both vessels were built in Scotland in 1880.

BELFAST, MAY 1911
This is another study of contrasts in maritime technology by W. A. Green. A wooden schooner
lies moored in Victoria Channel, while at Queen's Island the great steel hull of TITANIC, - *'the
highest attainment of naval architecture'* -is ready for launching.

ARDGLASS, CO. DOWN, c.1914

Ardglass has been a significant Ulster port since the middle ages. After hundreds of years of sailing vessels using the harbour, these lug-rigged herring drifters were the last to work under sail alone. Within a few years many of them had engines installed. Different regional boat types can be identified in the photograph. In the foreground two Scottish 'fifies' lie alongside the quay. Close to them is the nickey VICTORIA B233, built at St Ives Cornwall in 1870. Owned in Ardglass from 1910-26, she was fitted with an auxiliary motor in 1917. The light-coloured boats in the background are Portavogie nobbys. The nearest is the ALICE B318, built in 1911.

CURING HERRINGS, ARDGLASS, CO DOWN, c.1912

From about 1907 herring curing became a major commercial activity at Ardglass. In 1909, for example, nearly 9000 barrels and 3000 half barrels of cured herring were shipped out during the season. Men were employed as coopers, while women, mostly from Scotland and Donegal, gutted and packed the fish in salt.

KILKEEL, CO. DOWN, c.1918

The predominant boat type in the Kilkeel fleet was the west Cornish lugger and its Manx derivative, locally known as a nickey. Most were bought second hand, but a number were built at Kilkeel in the 1870s by the St Ives boatbuilder William Paynter. From 1903 onwards, second hand lug-rigged boats were also acquired from the east coast of Scotland. One of them is in the foreground of the photograph. She is the JEANNIE GARDINER, a small 45 ft zulu brought to Kilkeel in 1917 and shortly afterwards fitted with an engine. Ahead of her is the 52 ft nickey PEACE AND PLENTY, built at St Ives in 1886 and bought by Kilkeel owners in 1910. Although she was fitted with an auxiliary motor in 1917, her sailing rig was retained, as can be seen by the large mizzen lugsail drying in the light breeze.

NICKEY LEAVING KILKEEL, CO. DOWN, c.1915

This nickey setting off to the fishing grounds under sail is the UNCLE TOM N294. She was built at St Ives in 1883 and bought by James Mackintosh of Kilkeel in 1911. Like all nickeys, she could sail fast, work well to windward and was a fine sea boat. The dipping lugsail on the foremast and standing lugsail on the mizzen mast were handled by a 6-man crew, with a boy as an additional hand. In suitable sailing conditions a mizzen topsail, mizzen staysail and a big jib could also be set. Because the mizzen mast is stepped well aft, the mizzen sail is sheeted to a long boom projecting from the stern of the boat. After shooting the nets just after dusk, the tall foremast will be lowered and a small driving mizzen sail set to keep the boat head to wind while riding to her long train of drift nets.

CREW OF A NICKEY, KILKEEL, CO. DOWN, c.1920

Here the crew of the WATER LILY pose for the photographer while mending nets. From the left they are: Joe Collins, Charlie McCaver, Paddy Greenan, Charlie Maginness, John Ferguson and skipper Willie Cousins. He was also part-owner of the boat, which was bought at St Ives in 1914 for £150. WATER LILY was built there in 1896 and was regarded as one of the fastest luggers in Cornwall.

LANDING HERRINGS, KILKEEL, CO. DOWN, c.1920
A small crowd on the pier-head watches as herrings are landed from the nickey PEACE AND
PLENTY. Because of the state of the tide her skipper cannot bring her into the harbour. The
mizzen lugsail is set and the boat will probably lie off when the catch has been sent ashore.

NICKEY APPROACHING KILKEEL, CO. DOWN, c.1915

This Kilkeel nickey is the AMELIA JANE N387, owned by James McKee and James McKnight, who was also her skipper. Formerly the THEOPHILUS of St Ives, where she was built in 1882, the boat was renamed in 1914 when she joined the Kilkeel fleet. AMELIA JANE was sold to Balbriggan owners in 1920. The large dipping lug on the foremast acted as both foresail and mainsail and so was always set on the lee side of the mast. When the boat changed direction in relation to the wind, the sail had to be lowered, or dipped and hoisted again on the lee side.

SAIL AND MOTOR, KILKEEL, CO. DOWN, c.1918

Early auxiliary engines were low-powered and were used mainly to enable boats to manoeuvre in and out of harbour, or to replace the sweeps (oars) when there was no wind for the sails. It was only with the introduction of more powerful engines in the late 1920s that sails began to be abandoned. This photograph illustrates the advantage of engine-power, as the ketch is being towed out of the harbour by a motorised fishing boat. The boat on the left, MAID OF MOURNE N347, was one of the first motor assisted boats in the Kilkeel fleet. She was purpose-built in the Isle of Man in 1912 for Lord Newry. The boat on the right, EMU N62, a former Manx nobby, was first registered at Kilkeel in 1905.

SAIL AND MOTOR, GROOMSPORT, CO. DOWN, c.1914

Before 1914 Groomsport and neighbouring Donaghadee fishermen were installing auxiliary motors in their sailing and pulling yawls. Because of their low power and feared unreliability, these early engines were used to supplement sails rather than replace them. The boat setting the dipping lugsail, is the ANNIE WATERSON, one of the first purpose-built motor/sailing fishing boats at Groomsport. Completed in 1912, her innovative, smooth carvel hull contrasts with the clinker hulls of the older yawls.

ANNIE WATERSON, GROOMSPORT, CO. DOWN, 1914
Here is a closer view of Robert Waterson's 31 ft motor/sailing boat ANNIE WATERSON. Used for longline fishing, she was built in 1912 by Paddy McKeown of Whitla Street, Belfast. Reflecting the attitudes of her owner and builder, at a time when new technologies were replacing the old, ANNIE WATERSON, incorporated both innovation and conservatism in her design. She represents the local transition from an ancient reliance on sail and oar to the modern dependence on engine power.

R.N.L.B. WILLIAM & LAURA, DONAGHADEE LIFEBOAT, 1929
WILLIAM & LAURA, the first Donaghadee lifeboat, was also the first motor lifeboat in Ireland.
Stationed in the town from 1910-1934, she was a 43ft Watson class boat capable of 7 knots, with
sails augmenting engine-power. The lifeboat and her crew were photographed in September 1929
while standing by to render assistance to the Spanish ship ALBIA, which had run on to the Allen
Rock, off the coast of Co. Antrim.

CREW OF R.N.L.B. WILLIAM & LAURA, 1929
This photograph, taken at sea returning from the ALBIA, does not include the lifeboat's coxswain, Andy White. The volunteer crew were all Donaghadee fishermen. From the left they are; Tommy Simpson, Willie White, Alex Nelson, Alfie McWilliams, Sammy Nelson, Hugh Nelson, Bobby Simpson, and in front, Davy Nelson.

DONAGHADEE, CO. DOWN, 1939

Although sails were still used by local fishing boats in the late 1930s, they supplemented the more powerful engines which had replaced the first generation of auxiliary engines. The fishermen in these half-decked motor boats set a main standing lug when making a passage, and when working the longlines set a small mizzen lug. Sails can be seen in the nearest boat, COURAGEOUS, where James and Bob Bunting are baiting longlines for cod fishing. The motor winch, converted from the back axle of a motor car, was used when fishing for clams.

NEWCASTLE SKIFF JANE AT DUNDRUM, CO. DOWN, c.1930

Despite the widespread use of engines after the first world war, many small, open fishing boats continued to rely on sail and oar for propulsion. The 19ft, lug-rigged skiff JANE was one of several longline fishing boats which worked out of Newcastle. She was photographed at Dundrum after winning a race in the local regatta with her owner and skipper, James Smith, at the tiller. In Co. Down, south of St John's Point, double-ended, clinker-built open boats were referred to as skiffs, rather than yawls.

MOVILLE, LOUGH FOYLE, CO. DONEGAL, c.1930

Regattas were important social events for local fishermen, as they competed against each other in races for the working boats of the district. Here at Moville, the stationary committee boat contrasts with the lively motion of a Greencastle yawl, or 'drontheim', running before the wind under a full press of canvas. This is her racing rig of a jib and two spritsails, with a boom on the after sail to increase its efficiency. The local Moville boats were 26ft long, but this could be a 28ft 'westerd' (western) drontheim from Glengad on the Atlantic coast of Inishowen.

GREENCASTLE YAWL OR 'DRONTHEIM', MOVILLE, CO. DONEGAL, c.1930
Local fishermen stand in the shallows beside their double-ended, clinker-built open boat, known on the Inishowen Peninsula as a 'drontheim', deriving from the Norwegian port of Trondheim. The name acknowledges the Norwegian ancestry of this boat type, variants of which were common on all the coasts of Ulster. Together they represent the Irish element of a north-west European boatbuilding tradition, centred on Scandinavia, where there has been continuity of the double-ended clinker-building technique for more then 1000 years.

LOUGH NEAGH FISHING BOAT, CRANFIELD, CO. ANTRIM, c.1930

The great freshwater expanse of Lough Neagh is almost an inland sea. Sailing and rowing fishing boats had to be capable of working in conditions often more like the open sea then the sheltered waters of a lake. Lough Neagh boats were clinker-built and spritsail rigged on one or two masts. Unlike the lugsail, the spritsail was a rig of considerable antiquity. It was so called because of the diagonal sprit or spar which extended and supported the sail. The long oars pivoted on an iron pin or bolster, fitted as an outrigger on each side of the boat. The last Lough Neagh sailing boat worked until the 1960s and was acquired by the Ulster Folk and Transport Museum in 1973.

LOUGH NEAGH FISHERMAN, NEAR TOOME, CO. ANTRIM, c.1930

Eels, trout and pollan, a type of freshwater herring, were caught in nets and on baited lines. Here an eel fisherman, and probably his daughter, are preparing or 'pegging' the hundreds of hooks of a longline. When baited and set, the weighted longline will extend for a considerable distance over the bottom of the lough. The line is much lighter than that used by fishermen on the sea coast.

PORTAVOGIE, CO. DOWN, c.1930

Although Portavogie had become an important fishing village by the 1880s, the construction of a pier did not begin until 1900. The early harbour was tidal and, as can be seen in the photograph, 'legs' were fitted to the local nobbys to keep them upright when taking the ground. The FAMILY FRIEND B79, completed in June 1914 for Samuel Adair, was the last sailing nobby built in Portavogie. She was fitted with an auxiliary motor in 1917. VERVINE BLOSSOM B11 was built in Peel, Isle of Man in 1910 and bought by Hugh Adair in 1924. She was notable as an early purpose-designed motor/sailing nobby with a distinctive canoe-shaped stern.

PORTAVOGIE FISHERMEN, c.1925

This is an unusual formal studio portrait of two young Portavogie fishermen, wearing their best caps and knitted 'ganzies'. With dramatic side lighting on their faces and posed against a painted backcloth, Johnny McClements (seated) and William Donnan have been memorialised by a professional portrait photographer.

SCHOONER ALPHA, KILKEEL, CO. DOWN, c.1925

The 58 ton single topsail schooner ALPHA traded out of Kilkeel for over 50 years under different owners and skippers. Locally built in 1879 by William Paynter, she was eventually sold away to Scotland in the early 1930s. ALPHA had a reputation as a fast sailer and her shapely 75ft hull was pitch pine planking on oak frames. Here she is about to sail from the harbour with Captain James (Jimsey) Maginnis as skipper and owner.

SCHOONER MASTER, ANNALONG, CO. DOWN c.1925
Captain Hugh Chambers, known as 'The Major', was a famous Mourne schooner master. He was skipper of the DOROTHY, although this photograph is thought to have been taken on board the VOLANT. There is a great deal of interesting detail in the picture, and clearly Captain Chambers has been asked to pose for the photograph, as the schooner is in port.

NEWCASTLE, CO. DOWN, c.1935

Two sailing vessels are berthed in the harbour, against the majestic sweep of the Mourne Mountains. In the foreground, seamen on board the Annalong schooner LOCHRANZA CASTLE are in conversation with the owner of a half-decked motor skiff lying alongside. On the pier the driver of a horse and cart waits for discharging of the coal cargo to start. An approaching motor van is probably bringing ships supplies from the town. LOCHRANZA CASTLE, built in 1873, came to Annalong in 1917 and was fitted with an auxiliary engine in 1921. She was lost in November 1938 after going aground in the River Mersey during a gale.

KILKEEL, CO. DOWN, c.1929

Details in this photograph suggest a gradual decline in coastal sail at Kilkeel. An abandoned schooner hulk can be seen in the background, and on the quayside a 1-ton motor lorry reflects new road-based competition in the supply of goods to the locality. During the 1920s Kilkeel vessels, mostly fitted with auxiliary engines, worked economically in a Mourne-based trade with British and Irish ports. However when this contracted, with a fall in demand for granite, a decline in local shipowning was inevitable. The last Kilkeel schooner was sold in the mid 1930s.

ANNALONG, CO. DOWN, c.1935

This picturesque harbour, with a long tradition of seafaring, had the distinction of being the last schooner port in Ulster. Until the Second World War, three Annalong schooners, GOLDSEEKER, NELLIE BYWATER and VOLANT carried granite, potatoes, coal and other cargoes in the cross channel and coastal trades. They continued to earn a living for their local owners, skippers and crew, despite having to work in a changing maritime economy which favoured more efficient means of cargo handling, transport and distribution. Two of these schooners, the VOLANT and NELLIE BYWATER are in the foreground of the photograph. The 112 ton VOLANT, on the right, was built in 1875 and fitted with an auxiliary engine in 1926. She was broken up at Penrhyn near Falmouth in 1949.

ANNALONG, CO. DOWN, c.1930

Locals watch a wooden schooner leave the harbour on the starboard tack. Her old and heavily patched sails suggest careful management, although her square topsails have not been replaced with more economical fore and aft topsails. This schooner represents the final generation of shallow-draughted sailing vessels working in and out of small tidal harbours like Annalong.

POMMERN, OFF DONAGHADEE, CO. DOWN, 1938

During the 1920s and 30s, the world's last fleet of big square-rigged sailing ships was operated by the Finnish shipowner Gustav Erikson. He acquired many well known former British and German ships and sailed them profitably in the Australian grain trade. Belfast was one of their regular discharging ports and in the 1930s, ships of Erikson's fleet were the last commercial square-riggers to sail in local waters. Here the steel 4-masted barque POMMERN lies becalmed off Donaghadee with 4000 tons of wheat in her hold. She was built on the Clyde in 1903 and purchased by Erikson in 1922.

ON BOARD POMMERN, OFF DONAGHADEE, CO. DOWN, 1938

This view towards the bow of the ship from the poop, splendidly illustrates both her deck fittings and the mass of wire rigging needed to support the steel masts and control the sails of this large square-rigger. To be profitable, POMMERN sailed with a minimum crew and minimum maintenance, but clearly she was still smart and seamanlike. She was a product of industrial shipbuilding, quite different from the wooden schooners of Annalong.

POMMERN BECALMED OFF DONAGHADEE, CO. DOWN, 1938
Gustav Erikson operated his sailing ship fleet from the Baltic port of Mariehamn in the Aland Islands. Today POMMERN is preserved there intact and unchanged from the end of her working life in 1939.

PAMIR, BELFAST c.1935

The 4-masted barque PAMIR was bought by Erikson in 1931 from German owners. She was built in Hamburg in 1905, and remarkably made her last commercial voyage in 1949. Subsequently she was sold and converted to an auxiliary training ship under the German flag. In 1957 PAMIR was tragically lost at sea with all but 6 of her cadet crew.

LAWHILL, BELFAST, 1936

The steel 4-masted barque LAWHILL was photographed in the summer of 1936 after discharging a cargo of 4500 tons of wheat. She had left Port Lincoln in Australia on 7 March, and after arriving at Falmouth on 3 July was ordered to Belfast to discharge. Built at Dundee in 1892, LAWHILL was an early ship in the Erikson fleet, having been acquired in 1917. She was taken as a war prize by South African authorities in 1942 and was eventually broken up in 1957.

HERZOGIN CECILIE OFF BELFAST LOUGH, 1934

Although her steel hull shows the ravages of ocean voyaging, the HERZOGIN CECILIE was a beautiful 4-masted barque and the flagship of Gustav Erikson's fleet. Built in Bremerhaven in 1902 as a cargo-carrying schoolship, she was purchased by the Finnish shipowner in 1921. Sailing under ideal conditions HERZOGIN CECILIE set a record of 20 knots, but 16-18 knots were not unusual. In 1934, having discharged her grain cargo in Belfast, she sailed back to Port Lincoln in 91 days. Two years later the ship met her end, after running aground on the South Devon coast.

MOSHULU OFF BELFAST LOUGH, 1938

The 4-masted barque MOSHULU, 3120 gross tons, was built at Port Glasgow in 1904 for German owners and originally named KURT. After being laid-up for many years she was purchased by Gustav Erikson in 1935 and refitted for the grain trade. On 25 April 1938 MOSHULU sailed from Port Victoria, loaded with 4877 tons of wheat, and arrived at Falmouth on 23 August, 120 days later. Ordered to Belfast to discharge, she arrived off the coast in early September, when these splendid photographs were taken. Today MOSHULU is preserved in Philadelphia, albeit as a much altered restaurant ship.

MOSHULU OFF BELFAST LOUGH, 1938
In this remarkable photograph the overflying modern aircraft provides a powerful and unexpected
contrast with MOSHULU under sail - a technological hail and farewell!

GLOSSARY

Although technical terms have been kept to a minimum in this book, it has not been possible to dispense with them altogether. The following simplified list of seafaring terms might be helpful to the general reader.

barque: a three-masted vessel square-rigged on the fore and main masts and fore-and-aft rigged on the mizzen mast.

barquentine: a three-masted vessel square-rigged on the foremast and fore-and-aft rigged on the main and mizzen masts.

brig: a two-masted vessel square-rigged on both fore and main masts.

brigantine: a two-masted vessel square-rigged on the foremast and fore-and-aft rigged on the mainmast.

carvel-built: a method of wooden hull construction where flush planking is secured to a pre-erected skeletal frame.

clinker-built: a method of wooden hull construction where the hull is formed by overlapped and edge-joined planking, prior to the insertion of strengthening frames or ribs.

clipper: a vessel designed for fast sailing.

cutter: a fore-and-aft rigged single-masted vessel, often a yacht.

drifter: a fishing boat using drift nets to catch herring or mackerel.

fifie: a type of lug-rigged fishing boat, using drift nets, from the east coast of Scotland, particularly Fife.

fore-and-aft-rigged: the method of disposing the sails of a vessel so that they hang in the direction of her length (fore-and-aft), thus enabling the wind to act directly on either side of the sails.

full-rigged ship: a three masted vessel, square-rigged on the fore, main and mizzen head masts.

gabbart: a small single-masted trading vessel characteristic of the west cost of Scotland, particularly the Firth of Clyde.

gaff: a spar which extends the head or upper portion of a fore-and-aft sail.

ketch: a two-masted vessel fore-and-aft rigged on both main and mizzen masts.

lugsail: in general a lug is a four-sided fore-and-aft sail suspended from a yard.

mizzen: a relatively small mast or associated sail at the after end of a vessel.

oakum: unpicked natural fibre rope used for caulking or stopping leaks in wooden vessels.

poop: a covering deck on the after part of a vessel.

schooner: a two-masted vessel, fore-and-aft rigged on both fore and mainmasts and often carrying square topsails on the foremast. A three-masted schooner also had a mizzen mast.

sheer: the curved line which the deck of a vessel makes when viewed from the side.

smack: a fore-and-aft rigged single-masted vessel, either a small trader or a fishing boat.

spritsail: a four-sided fore-and-aft sail extended by a diagonal sprit or spar.

square-rigged: the method of disposing the sails of a ship so that they hang across the vessel and allow the wind to act directly only on their after side.

yard: a spar suspended from a mast for the purpose of extending a sail.

zulu: a type of lug-rigged fishing boat, using drift nets, from the north east coast of Scotland. So called after the Zulu War of 1879.

FURTHER READING

The undernoted books and many others on various aspects of maritime history may be consulted in the Museum Library by arrangement with the Librarian.

Anderson, E. M., *Sailing ships of Ireland* (Dublin 1951, reprinted Coleraine 1984)

Anderson, R., *The port of Coleraine* (Coleraine 1977)

Anderson, R and Wilson, I., *Ships and quaysides of Ulster* (Belfast 1990)

Cecil, T., *The harsh winds of Rathlin - stories of Rathlin shipwrecks* (Coleraine 1990)

Cooke, S., *The maiden city and the western ocean* (Dublin c. 1950)

C.T.A.R.A., *Down the quay, A history of Dundalk harbour* (Dundalk c.1988)

Derby, W., *The tall ships pass* (Newtown Abbot 1970, revised ed.)

Donnelly, D., *On Lough Neagh's shores* (Galbally 1986)

Finch, R., *Sailing craft of the British Isles* (London 1976)

Forde, F., *Maritime Arklow* (Dun Laoghaire 1988)

Gilligan, H., *A history of the port of Dublin* (Dublin 1988)

Greenhill, B., *The merchant sailing ship* (Newton Abbot 1970)

Greenhill, B., *The merchant schooners* (2 vols) (Newton Abbot 1968, revised ed.)

Greenhill, B., *The life and death of the merchant sailing ship* (London 1980)

Ireland, de Courcy J., *Ireland's sea fisheries: a history* (Dun Laoghaire 1981)

Ireland, de Courcy J., *Ireland and the Irish in maritime history* (Dun Laoghaire 1986)

Lubbock, B., *The last of the windjammers* (2 vols) (Glasgow 1970, reprint)

MacGregor, D., *Merchant sailing ships 1850-1875* (London 1984)

McCaughan, M., *Steel ships and iron men* (Belfast 1989)

McCaughan, M., and Appleby, J. (eds), *The Irish Sea, aspects of maritime history* (Belfast 1989)

McKee, E, *Working boats of Britain* (London 1983)

Maddock, J., *Rosslare harbour past and present* (Rosslare 1986)

March, E., *Sailing drifters* (Newton Abbot 1969)

Moss, M., and Hume, J.R., *Shipbuilders to the world* (Belfast 1986)

Mourne Observer, *Sailing ships of Mourne* (Newcastle 1971)

Newby, E., *The last grain race* (London 1956)

Pearson, P., *Dun Laoghaire - Kingstown* (Dublin 1981)

Rees, J., and Charlton, L., *Arklow, last stronghold of sail* (Arklow 1985)

Rossiter, N., *Wexford Port - a history* (Wexford 1989)

Scott, R., *The Galway hookers* (Dublin 1983)

Sweetnam, R., and Nimmons, C., *Port of Belfast* (Belfast 1985)

Wilson, I., *Shipwrecks of the Ulster coast* (Coleraine 1979)

Young, J., *A maritime and general history of Dungarvan* (Dungarvan c. 1980)

ACKNOWLEDGEMENTS

I should like to record my grateful thanks to all those who have made this book possible. In particular I am indebted to the following people who have contributed to the work of the Museum by donating or lending photographs and often providing valuable information about them (plate references in brackets):

Mr A. Armstrong (45)

Mrs E. Boyd (71)

Mr V. Chambers (117)

Mrs D. Corcoran (44)

Mr T. Roger Corry, chairman, James P. Corry Holdings Ltd (30-35)

Mr W. Doherty (106, 107)

Mr D. Donnan (111)

Mrs P. Duncan (7)

Mr P. Flood (51)

Mr J. French (81)

Mr R. Gifford (58)

Mr W. Gilmore (36)

Mrs A. Loane (64-67)

Mrs E. McBride (80)

Mr E. McCreedy (70)

Mrs Morrison (118, 120, 125)

Mourne Observer (84, 85, 96, 113)

Alderman S. Neeson (6)

Mr R. Palmer (87)

Dr P. Robinson (122)

Mr W. Shaw (121)

Mr J. Simpson (102, 103)

the late Mr J. Smith (105)

the late Mr K. Smyth (52-57, 60, 61, 68, 73-75)

Mr J. T. Steele (86)

Mr D. Swain (123)

Mr J. Waterson (69)

Mr I. Workman (124)

For information and assistance in my researches, thanks are also due to Mr D. MacPolin, Mrs S. Speers of the Ulster Museum and Mr M. K. Stammers of Merseyside Maritime Museum.

In addition to photographs made available by individuals, the book has drawn on collections in the Museum's Photographic Archive. These are:

Belfast Telegraph Collection (104)

de Ros Collection (frontispiece, 18-20)

General Collection (8, 9, 29, 43, 47, 59, 72, 76, 78, 79, 97, 112, 116)

Green Collection (77, 82, 83, 88, 89-95, 98-101)

Harland & Wolff Collection (10-17, 28, 37-39, 46, 48-50, 62, 63)

Holden Collection (2-5)

Swanston Collection (21-27, 40-42)

I am most appreciative of the help and support given by my colleagues in the Department of Photography at the Ulster Folk and Transport Museum. Thanks are due to Kenneth Anderson for advice in searching the archive and to Alan McCartney and George Wright for producing the selected photographs. Finally I should like to thank my office colleagues, Mrs Lorraine Lawrence and Mrs Hilary Connor, for typing the manuscript with efficiency and forbearance.